Out of the Ashes

A Collection of Poems

Discovering Purpose and Power in Pain

Victoria (Tori) Martinez

Out of the Ashes: A Collection of Poems Discovering Purpose and Power in Pain

 First Edition - Made in the USA.

Contents

Introduction		**6**
Chapter one	I Am Woman	**8**
Chapter Two	Muchos Colores (Many Colors)	**38**
Chapter Three	In the Fires of Suffering	**57**
Chapter Four	Healing Humanity	**73**

Chapter One – *I Am Woman*, is a collection of poems that hold my lived experience of being female, our tenderness, our fury, our fire, and our light. These poems are shaped by the women who have shaped me, loved me, challenged me, and taught me how to survive in ways both seen and unseen.

Chapter Two – *Muchos Colores,* or *Many Colors,* is a tender unfolding of poems rooted in lived experience, where culture, ethnicity, and multiracial identity are held with reverence and honesty. These pieces move through memory and belonging, honoring the beauty of layered heritage and the quiet strength it takes to live between worlds, fully and unapologetically

Chapter Three – *In the Fires of Suffering* holds moments of struggle, where words come softly. These poems don't rush to explain but offer time to sit within pain and honor our grief and endurance.

Sometimes we just need words to remind us we are not alone in our suffering.

Chapter Four – *Healing Humanity* offers whispers of hope and faith. The poems in this chapter work to unravel the tangle of thoughts and experiences to find a path toward spiritual, mental, cultural and emotional healing.

Chapter One

I am Woman

MY CULTURAL INHERITANCE

I am from brown dirt
and red clay.
I am from the acequias
flowing with life-giving water
from the top of the mountain,
above the tree line of green pines,
to the valley floor of alfalfa fields.

I am from my Abuelita's cocina
filled with the aromas of tortillas y frijoles,
and from my mama's garden
of peas and papas.

I am from the mighty river
where La Llorona cries

for the loss of her children,

her language,

her culture,

her home.

I am from the painted canvas

of Apache feathers

and Ute necklaces that adorn my mother's mother.

Whose eyes are filled with sadness

and hold many secrets.

I am from all the corn mothers before me.

The givers of life,

the dreamers of dreams,

the dancers and painters,

the writers and maestras,

the sculptors that portray the essence of

la feminino y las mujeres sabias.

I am from a history of sorrow and resilience.

From a past of joy and pain.

From a culture as colorful as the rainbow,

daring me to be brave enough to immortalize its stories

in black ink on a white page.

THE WOMAN'S GARDEN

When she was a child, a man she called father planted a wondrous seed - the love of art, into the garden of her heart.

When she was a teenager, a woman she called mother planted another - persistence, Si se Puede.

She went through life's trials and joys, sowing seeds every day, in all those simple little ways.

As a woman, she was hurt by a man who took and then walked away. Leaving seeds of doubt, shame, and regret sown so very deep. She would catch herself in pain, tears would flow, bad dreams would come, and sometimes she couldn't explain.

Then one day the woman looked within and found the seeds had grown; a garden in full bloom she now owned.

She saw beauty beyond her wildest dreams. She smelled fragrant perfume, sweeter than anything she'd ever known. But she also saw thorns and weeds, a darkness that was trying to uproot the beauty of her private garden.

The roots were deep and the weeds were many, but with each weed that she removed she could feel the pain go too.

Each root a dream lost from shame, each weed a word carelessly spoken out of fear or blame, each thorn a pain inflicted that she had not let go of.

And when the deed, though hard, was done the woman arose and found she'd changed. Now strong, safe, and forever brave. She felt consumed with love, joy, and peace, at last she knew she felt complete.

Now the woman sees a rainbow in the garden of her heart.

She guards its gates with tender, watchful care.

Always vigilant about who enters.

Always careful of who sows seeds there.

WOMEN OF MANY COLORS

My grandmother used to say, that God was the great chef.

That he baked the white woman only a little,

That he baked the black woman for a long time,

but the Hispanic and Native women, he cooked just right –

and we came out of the oven with beautiful brown skin.

But she emphasized,

that although we all came out of the oven different colors

we were all still the same cookie.

Some brown women say, “I am Hispanic!”

Others say, “I am Latina!”

Yet others claim to be Mexicana,

Or Indio-Hispano, Puerto Rican, Columbian,

Or Dominican.

We have many names for our many identities.

So claim the name that's right for you.

Claim the name of the identity you choose.

What matters is,

that our stories are told

of women's days

and what women

know.

Of women's work,

in women's worlds.

By women's voices,

in women's words!

LA COCINA (THE KITCHEN)

She stood at the stove, stirring ever so slow.

The papas y frijoles in a warm, gentle glow.

The rich aroma curled through the air,

A silent call for familia to gather there.

La cocina is where the stories were told.

Plans for the future,

and traditions of old.

Comida, our sustenance.

We all need to eat to survive.

A feast of many colors, from many hands it came.

Each dish a different story.

Each aroma a piece of heritage proclaimed.

New friends would bring new dishes.

Old friends would bring new news.

Never a moment for silence.

Never a moment to be still.

La cocina was the playground for a battle of wills.

En la cocina I learned:

> To read the Bible and stand with grace.
>
> To always be unafraid.
>
> To make round tortillas while hands keep pace.
>
> To speak with courage, strong and true.
>
> And to honor my elders and give them their due.

En la cocina we didn't just prepare our children's food.

We carefully crafted their character too!

En la cocina

Standing wise and true

were our Mamas, Tias, y Abuelas too,

Their voices held the power.

Their words fanned the flames.

Their wisdom dealt justice, as they called us by name.

As a curious child, la cocina was bright.

A place full of magic,

Of warmth and light.

A mystery deep, a love so strong.

The heart of the home, that made us belong.

CHRONIC WARRIOR

It was but yesterday that I was

strong as the sea,

graceful and free,

slender and spree.

But today the mirror whispers to me

Of bending the knee.

For my step has slowed.

My sway now bears a heavier load.

My form, once bestowed with curves, now rounded.

I am no longer free.

And I can't help but agree with this image before me.

Yet my spirit boldly sings to me

I love you now, unconditionally.

I'll nourish you and help you grow.

And cherish all you are,

not who I used to know.

For I found beauty

in my rounded curves.

Rest in the fog

for my fragile nerves.

Resilience that came

in the darkest hours.

It brings color to my canvas,

and truth to the ink on my page.

I've become a warrior empowered

to fight a battle none can see.

I am changed by what has happened

Yet I will not let it reduce me.

THE BRAVEST SOLDIERS

The bravest
soldiers
that ever were
never thought of
themselves so.

They trudged on
each day,
and woke each
morn, praying it be
better than the last.

They battled not with sword or gun,
or the mighty pen.
Nor in the fields, or office towers

used by modern men.

But deep within a woman's heart,
which was wounded, and had bled.

With inner turmoil
and outward grace
she fought off tears,
picked up her tools of trade
and marched into the battlefield of motherhood.
Not knowing her own strength.

No squad of soldiers to back her up.
yet no wavering of her stance.
Though the battles seemed so many
she remained steadfast to the end.

Though the battles seemed so long.
She fought with all her might;
to save her lost child,
to heal a wounded heart,
to guide a wondering teenager,
and mold an eager mind.

I say thank you!
To all those brave soldiers.

To those who may never have been thanked.

To all those mighty mothers, step-mothers, and spiritual mothers

who remained faithful to the grave!

GRANDMOTHER

I watch the curl of her lips,

the swing of her hips,

as she commands the room.

It's the tone of her voice,

the way she lifts her
arms,

the glimmer in her
eyes

that captivates you.

Word, after spoken
word,

she pulls you into
her world.

A world she creates,

right before your eyes,

using only her words.

You are mesmerized by her every move,

this modern Scheherazade.

She spins a tale of old,

a poem unfolds,

a history is remembered,

her power - a treasure.

The past, present, future

all within reach.

It takes her but a moment to transport you there.

With the flick of her hand,

or a change in her tempo,

she moves you from darkness to light.

She stands, and you quiver.
She steps towards you, and you sigh.
She is a giant among women,
an owl in flight.

She’s a keeper of culture,
a bringer of her dreams.
She’s a force of nature,
this storyteller.

It’s her long black hair flowing in the breeze.
It’s the sway of her brightly colored dress, as she dances past you.
It’s the scent of the fields still resting on her breasts.

It’s all of that,

and what you cannot see,

that my grandmother has passed on to me.

WE RISE (inspired by Maya Angelou's poem "Still I Rise")

From the beginning, we were never meant to rise.

We were held down by chains,

made of men's sexism masked as chivalry.

In the annals of history, women were just considered property.

Our stories overshadowed by his privileged accomplishments.

Yet we rise!

To educate a woman was just a waste of time. Yet that did not stop us from broadening our minds.

We rose through the halls of science, to achieve the Nobel prize,

We marched the streets on capital hill to win the right to vote,

And dared to venture through the skies.

Yes we rise!

We rise when we dare to step into the marble house and claim the power monopolized by men.

We rise from centuries of cumulative inequality, from the ashes of second-class citizenry, we rise.

We rise above the decades of stereotypical lies. Soaring closer to our dreams we rise. On the wings of hope for future generations of women we rise.

Eyes glistening with pride, on the shoulders of giant women we rise.

We rise! We rise!

THE DOUBLE BIND

They say to be sexy
But not too sexy

They say to be honest
But not too blunt

They say don't be emotional
Or else you're a bitch

Get married they say
But divorce is a failure

Have children, it's your duty
But not too many

Be beautiful – that's the goal
We shouldn't be too heavy
Or wear too much makeup
We don't want white hair

Be perfect
after all you're a woman…

I AM

I am an instrument of change

I am a womb of awakening

I am an arrow of
acceleration

I am a voice of purpose

I am a window of
heaven

I am exploring my
power

I am reinventing my life

I am reimagining the
future

I am stronger

I am braver

I am bolder

I am softer and wiser

I am water, nature, sky

I am universe

I am night and day

I am dark and light

I am joy

I am fury

I am love

I am anger

I am woman

CIRCLE OF WOMEN

Mother, Sister, Aunt, Friend

I am wrapped in this circle of women

Covered by their wisdom

Surrounded by their grace

Filled with their strength

Grandmother, Neighbor, Teacher

I am growing in a circle of women

Taught how to sing

Shown how to sew

Guided by their truth

Writer, Poet, Singer, Artist

I am lifted by the circle of women

Dancing to their rhythms and rhyme

Drawn to every story

Inspired by their powerful lives

Activist, Advocate, Feminist

I am empowered by circles of women

Given a voice

Lifted on their shoulders

Driven to action

Round and round

Mary go round

This circle of strong

Brave women

The circle of life

Mary gives life

As Eve once did

To a circle of loud

Powerful women

I shout and I cry

I laugh and I praise

With my own

Little circle of women

WHEN YOU GROW UP

If you grow up being told you're too bossy, too loud, too demanding.

> What they mean, but don't know how to say, is you're a leader, you're strong, you know what you want and that's a good thing.

If you grow up being called a nerd, a book worm, teacher's pet, a brown noser.

> It just means you dared to venture into the black ink of a good book, to take the path few follow, to expand your mind, the most precious part of you.

If you grow up and the love of your life makes you feel like a failure, less than…

> Then they are not THE ONE to understand your high standards, to support your big dreams, to learn from past mistakes, or grow with you along the way.

If you grow up to feel lost in the mist over the fields

Just keep moving, the mist will fade and you will find yourself.

If you grow up looking for love in all the wrong places

Remind yourself that your greatest love has been there all along, looking at you from the mirror.

If you grow up wanting to crawl out of your own dark skin, or despising your thick thighs

Look at those little miracles you tuck into bed each night and know they're worth it!

If you grow up to regret those bad decisions, the roads not taken

Know that life is about the journey, not the destination you're still traveling and can change direction.

Because when you grow up

You will be the author of your own life!

Chapter Two

Muchos Colores

(Many Colors)

UNI-VERSE ONE-SONG

In the forest sat a wolf alone, and as he looked longingly into the night sky he began to cry.

From his mouth arose the song of a wolf's howl. As he sang he drew his kind to him. They came from the North, from the South, the East and the West. Each wolf adding his voice to the rest.

One song they sang, in unity, though each one's voice was quite unique. They told a story of a vast unending sky, under which they dwelt both day and night, of a universe so grand they could not describe.

On they sang into the night until the dawn brought morning's light. When its rays touched their brow, a wolf no longer did there dwell.

But in the sky an eagle called, and from its mouth arose an eagle's song. His song drew his kind to him, and their wings stretched across the sky, as in unity they sang their eagle's cry. On they sang throughout the morn, until the sun rose to its peak, and then no Eagle did there speak.

On the water stood a man, and not a word did he speak and yet he drew his kind to him.

A sound rose up throughout the land, as each human boldly took their stand. On they stood throughout the day, and not a word did any say.

Clearer still was what they did, as each one took the hand next to them.

Then arose a trumpet sound, then a harp was heard aloud, and then a drum was added in. All this came from their hearts - within.

As a wolf, an eagle, and a human sang one song of creator's plan.

STILL SURVIVING

When our homes were burnt to the ground, we were not meant to survive.

When our women were taken, and our children ripped from mother's arms to boarding school buildings, our deaths came in the form of broken bodies, lost language, forbidden culture, and invisible futures.

The land, our mother, seized and sold to the highest bidder, we were meant to starve, fall from sickness, and weaken through heartbreak.

We were forbidden to sing, dance, wear our feathers, or smoke our pipes, because we were never meant to survive.

Yet the Indian is still here! We are still alive, we have survived, we are survivors.

We are called the red man. But it is our anger, our fury, and most of all our determination that others see as red. It is our unbreakable relationship with nature they envy. It is our bond with each other they fear. It is our connection to creator they desire.

We have not disappeared silently into the history books. For most of our history is unwritten.

We are a living history, a living culture, a vibrant people. Living in our own lands surrounded by many colors of immigrants, we now welcome as neighbors, some are even friends.

But they don't know, or don't care that their home was built on the blood and bodies of my people.

They just don't know, and may never understand why I say, I am still surviving.

It is not that my people's memories are long lasting.

Nor is it that we have not forgiven.

It is difficult for one to let go of the past,

if the battle has not yet passed.

WHO AM I?

The words of society ring in my ears daily.

As a child they made me wonder who I really am.

Am I brown or red?

Must I really choose only one color,

one ethnicity, one identity?

What part of me, what part of my family,

What part of our stories should be seen?

I am torn between worlds!

I am of a conquered native people.

I am of those who conquered for a time

Pora dominar esta tierra

only to be conquered themselves.

I am of people who have lost

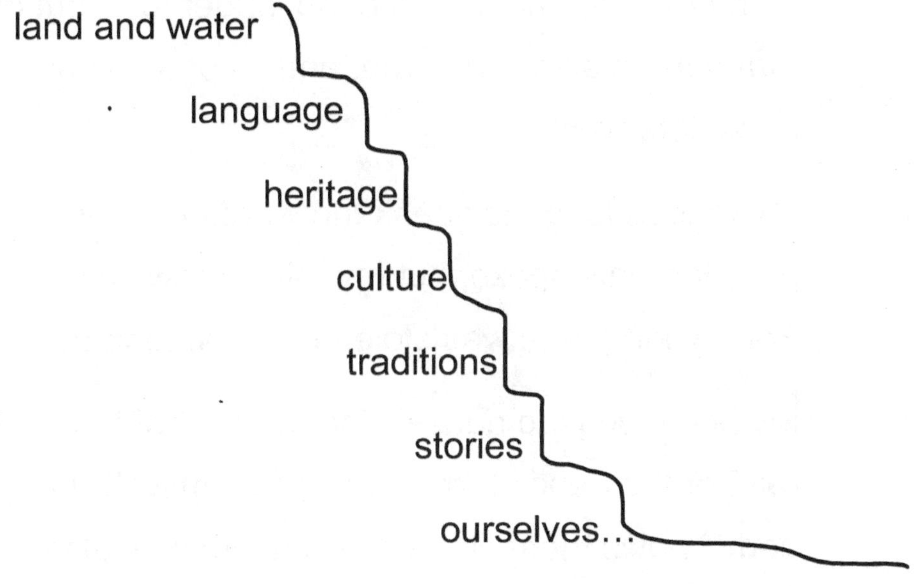

I am of slaves and slave owners.

The dominated and the dominators.

The conquered and the conquerors.

I am torn, divided, longing to be whole!

Longing for words to express my duality, my colors, my complexities.

The universe whispers multiracial, multi-passionate, intersectional, but who is listening…

I long for a harmonious life, no longer torn, but one that honors all of who I am, and all of who my ancestors were.

My tongue longs to speak the words that my grandparents spoke, but my mind knows them not. For my language was stolen from me long ago.

My body longs to dance. The dance that brings the rain, or the dance that celebrates family. But my body knows them not, for my culture was also stolen.

Without those things my own people reject me. They say I am not Indian enough, I am not Hispanic enough.

So, who am I, really.

Am I brown or red?

And why do others insist that I must choose only one?

If I refuse to choose what will they do?

What could they say?

I am who I am either way.

CORN MOTHERS

With a sacred wisdom and warrior-like courage

With simple acts of bravery and generosity

Through many talents

And filled with love.

They reach through the complexities of time and space

To heal the scars of humanity's past.

Corn Mothers

Encourage growth through creativity

Because They create life.

Corn Mothers

In their many shapes, sizes, and colors.

They represent the

strength

determination

and beauty

of all women.

Corn Mothers

Dare to restore harmony

By simply sharing

their journeys toward

accessibility

equity

And enlightenment.

Corn Mothers

honor the past

to create a brighter future.

They tend to the earth and all its children.
They hold our sacred places
within the safety of their bosom.

Corn Mothers

are the keepers of culture.
Their truth - teaches us humility.
Their works - gather the community.
Their words - impart wisdom.
Their hands - pass on tradition.

Though not perfect- for no human could be,
their Intertwining lives leave a powerful legacy
a lasting tapestry for seven generations to come.

THE SILENT STORY OF ADDICTION

It started as a child, being teased for her brown skin.

It continued as a teenager,

when they said her clothes became too wild,

when really her hormones

just forced out her hips and breasts a little too early

and her mama couldn't afford to buy a bigger size.

The boys at school weren't taught not to look

And the teachers called her - a distraction,

Then he stole a kiss,

And a touch,

until he touched a little too much…

But she never cried, she held it all in,

never told anyone what he did.

Instead, her numbing of choice was easily obtained.
She simply told the doctor the pain wouldn't fade.
He'd hand her script after script
and she'd down them like candy.

She never noticed the change in her stance,
The angry outbursts became her normal trance.
The lying and stealing her daily trade.
It didn't matter that she never knew where she'd awake.

She lost her dignity, her name, then her children.

But she never cried,
- that is, until she lost a limb.

Everyone thought it was a blessing in disguise.

Maybe she'd straighten her act out this time.

But somewhere along her dark and lonely road,

she had already lost all hope. And started to take that no-good dope.

No matter what her family said, or did,

she just never let their love in.

No matter how many chances they gave,

her response was always the same.

Even after all the times she'd been arrested.

That crack-ed road

stole her beauty,

her potential,

her hope.

For although she's alive, we know she's not truly living.

Addiction does not discriminate,

It didn't care that she was a daughter, a sister, a mother.

But we should not lay down this fight.

We should not let her "go silently into that dark night".

We should fight and fight and fight, as long as there is breath to breathe.

Fight for her freedom from that zombie-like existence.

Fight for the freedom of worry, for her mother.

Fight for the freedom from late nights, for her father searching the streets for his lost daughter.

Too many families bearing the guilt and the shame
for not liberating that child in pain.

Yet, the grip of addiction holds an entire community down.
It falls deeper and deeper into the hole
of darkness and shame

But the burden of change - no one wants to share.
So, these families bear it in sorrow, alone.

As a legacy of poverty
And layers of traumas
that our man-made
systems create,

Silently

condemns

another daughter

or son

to the grave!

Chapter Three

In the Fires of Suffering

DEATH CAME CALLING

Death came calling suddenly
but I would not let him in

so onward I go
though struggling along life's road
smiling through the pain

Hair turned white
my body slowed
my prayers stretched to heaven

Death came calling once again
but I would not bow my head

I fought the good fight

though the battle was grueling

love's wings held me tight
and faith saw me through each night

Tiny hands wrapped around mine
remind me of why
I fight that good fight

I reluctantly
put away my labor

for a brief moment
paused in leisure
enjoying the company
of family and friends

Hair now gone
body weakened
crying out to heaven
Death called again
this time, a welcomed friend
we travel together
hand in hand
as he escorts me to heaven

I leave you now
separation is temporary
death is but a drop
in the sea of eternity
I'll patiently wait
till once again
we can share an embrace
reuniting at the gates of heaven…

ANGER

Anger beckons at my door,
won't you let me in?
Never, is my reply,
for you are not my friend.

You wish to start a war, and you bring with you your troops; bitterness, regret, suspicion, and envy too. I will not fall prey to your fancy play on words.

Anger only knows the past
and flares up old wounds.

The defense of choice
is faith, hope, and truth.

I see this not as a battle

one fights in the dark of night,

but a gathering of truth

to which one brings the light!

For there is a greater story

Deeper than your fleeting touch

That story may be painful

But I search for it till dusk

And once it is uncovered

I know that I'll be free

Dwelling in the light of who I'm meant to be…

DEPRESSION

Darkness engulfs

I'm swimming in a pool of brown tar

oh bed - soft prison

holding captive

my aching head

my bleeding heart

my torn spirit

daylight do not come

my eyes red and swollen

no tears left to cry

body bone dry

phone don't ring

mouth won't speak

no words can describe

the depth and breadth of my sorrow

my silent plea - unheard

days melt into weeks

weeks stretch into months

falling down the rabbit hole

lost - like Alice in Wonderland

In that place of chaos and confusion

I discovered

Love - my ladder

Hope – my strength

Time – my healer

Slowly the ache fades

Beat by slow, determined beat

my heart is mended

Defiant, I stitched up my spirit

Climbed into the light

And rejoined the human race.

WHEN LIFE IS:

Challenging: Rise to the occasion and shine

Hurtful: Forgive and learn from the experience

Exciting: Enjoy the ride

Full of responsibilities: Fulfill them, then go beyond

Dull: Choose to create something fresh

Full of people who say you can't: Prove them wrong

Full of hate: Choose to spread love

Stuck in a rut: Find a new way out

Great: Be thankful

Full of trials: Hand them over to a higher power

Full of choices: Consider the results before you choose

Boring: Change perspective

Going too fast: Catch up to it, or make it slow down

Full of boundaries: Tear them down, it's not a solid wall

Sunny: Take in the beauty of it all

Rainy, cloudy, or sad: Talk to a friend

Is being life: It never hurts to pray

TWO PEOPLE

There are
two types of people
in society today

There are those who
say the nature of
humanity is cruel.

They focus on what's
wrong and see no
change in sight.

There are those who
say humanity is
capable of great things.

They focus on what's
right and good and try
to do the same.

There are
two types of people
with vastly differing
views.

Of these two types of
people,
which one,
my friend,
are you?

LIFE IS

Life is full of a wide range of circumstances.

Each one is neither good nor bad.

It simply is a circumstance.

Wise people see each one

as an appointment with God,

that leads to change.

Disillusioned people see them

as a trial,

that leads to

disappointment or pain.

Life is full of

a wide range of choices.

No choice is ever good or bad

it simply is, a choice.

Wise people see the results

of their choice,

before the choice is made.

Foolish people

rush to make a choice,

and then regret

the choices that they made.

YOU ARE WORTHY

When rain begins to fall,
to water the earth,
does the tree cry out
“no I’m not worthy to drink?”

When the sun begins to shine,
to light the earth,
does the dove cry out,
“no I’m not worthy to see day?”

Why then, when life reaches out with love
to give us joy, peace, or wealth
does humanity cry out,
“no I’m not worthy!”

For it is said when we choose to hate.

It is said when we choose to forget ourselves.

It is said when we fear to die.

And it is said when we fear to live.

Chapter Four

Healing Humanity

TODAY I LAUGHED

Today I laughed. I laughed because laughter came when I needed it the most. I laughed because laughter is the greatest medicine.

Today I laughed the kind of laughter that frees the soul. My soul was in chains for so long. I laughed because I saw joy and it was God. I laughed because now I know that God laughs too.

Today I laughed so hard that I fell on the floor in ecstasy!

I laughed for all the times I would not allow laughter to come. I laughed for all the blessings I never noticed, but can now be thankful for. I laughed for all the tears that came during the struggles, that really did change my life for the better.

Today I laughed until my stomach ached, and it was a good ache. I laughed so hard that I cried, a cry of joy like no other.

Today I laughed, and the sound reached deep into my past and healed my wounds.

Today I laughed because I found myself. I laughed because I found peace. I laughed because now I can love again. I laughed because I chose to see the good.

I laughed as I thought of my friends, and all the fun times we shared. I laughed because I remembered their laughter. I laughed because time and distance can never separate a spiritual bond.

Today I laughed for all the lessons learned. For all my family and friends, because now I know they are, and always have been in God's hands and not mine.

Today I laughed for all the circumstances that are to come, bad or good. I laughed because it's not the circumstance that determines my quality of life, but how I choose to process them in my thoughts.

Today I laughed.

I laughed because I wanted to.

I laughed because I needed to.

I wrote about my laughter and it made others laugh too.

Because today I laughed for truth!

CONNECTEDNESS

There is a string that connects all things.
Although this string cannot be seen.

Some call it energy, or fate.
I call it power, God, and grace.

It's everywhere, in everything,
and it cannot be contained.

It unites the sparrow with the tree.
It unites my hand with pen and ink.
It unites me with you, and you with me.

Time does not limit it,
for it is time, and time is it.

It unites thought to man's mind.

It unites molecules,

to create water, to sustain life.

It unites air to lungs, so we might breathe.

It is everywhere, in everything.

Even though it can't be seen.

It is everywhere, in everything.

Even if you choose not to believe.

HEALING PLACES

There is a place of solitude.
Where I find rest from the world.

There is a place of memories.
Where I am surrounded by my favorite things.

In this place:
The rushing river shapes the stones.
The sound of the breeze dances among the trees.
The sunset lasts forever.
And I soak it all in from the mountain top above it all.

There is a place of peaceful surrender.
In a little church within,

to have conversations with God.

There is a place of cleansing forgiveness.

In the river of life,

at the base of a rushing waterfall.

That washes away my worries and fears.

These are my places for healing.

The places that set me free.

Healing places,

God created just for me.

THE WAY TO HEAVEN'S WINDOW

As a child

viewing life through a colored windowpane

Unable to see life

in all its splendor, was I

But a ray of light began to seep, slowly, gently,

piercing through that darkened windowpane.

I felt Love's first touch upon my brow,

warm and welcoming.

Each day I sat at that window

desiring more,

hoping for something new

to break through that crack so minute.

But hope is not in vain,

and dreams really can come true.

For desire itself melted away the gloom from that windowpane,

so I could see.

Eyes opened.

I saw tears, fear, and pain.

But heart renewed I saw past that, deeper than that.

I saw faith, joy, and peace. I saw love in all its glory.

Each day I sat at that window.

Gazing out at all that passed by.

Desperately desiring more.

Hoping for something new to step into view.

But hope is not in vain.

And dreams, though they may change, can still come true.

For desire itself shattered that windowpane.

I bravely stepped out, ventured forth, and experienced what I had seen.

I experienced tears, fear, and pain.

But past that, deeper than that,

I experienced faith, joy, and peace.

I encountered love and dared to let it in.

Upon my daily walk I see many darkened windows.

Closed and lonely.

Full of unexpected treasures.

Treasures locked inside.

And I desperately desire more.
I hope for something new
to venture out
of that soon-to-be opened window of heaven.

But hope is not in vain,
and dreamers do awake.
Each day I know it is so.
Each day another dreamer dares to venture forth.

I know, the way to heaven's window.
For desire itself draws them forth.
And they too know,
the way to heaven's window.

Each day we look inside that open window.

We find ourselves face-to-face with truth.

And we shout out in every way we can,

the way through heaven's window

MY GLIMPSE OF JOY

My gaze met with elderly eyes today, as I was driving. Frozen in a state of blue sadness, she smiled at me, for no reason. And I caught a glimpse of joy.

An encounter with a child today led to a hug, for no reason. Me, a stranger to him, and he a stranger to me. And I caught a glimpse of joy.

A visit with a dear friend on her birthday, I presented her with a gift that evoked a cry of delight. And I caught a glimpse of joy.

A conversation with a sibling on the phone. She just had a baby boy. His voice heard for the first time, so sweet and new, so fresh and beautiful. And I caught a glimpse of joy.

A gift received - nothing traditional nor romantic. Nothing to make the giver feel good, or to make a good impression. A gift only I could love, and only the giver knew I would. And I caught a glimpse of joy.

Acceptance expressed in words, “I love you.” Such an unexpected phrase but welcome all the same. To see a smile on her face, and the sparkle in her eyes. And I caught a glimpse of joy.

The privilege to feed those who have none and serve them when it’s needed. The opportunity to witness gratitude and share stories. The ability to intertwine lives for a brief moment. And I caught a glimpse of joy.

To help restore a marriage that was once dead. To get to see love born again. Being in the right place at the right time. And I caught a glimpse of joy.

I received a letter today. Full of compliments, encouragements, and advice. It made me laugh and it made me cry. And I caught a glimpse of joy.

I read God’s word and prayed last night. And in the midst of that, I met Jesus – the Christ. His word told me that he loved me, and that he always has. His word revealed my purpose and said it all fits into his plan. And finally, yes finally, I know who joy really is!

I LIKE

I like when someone can touch my heart.

When their words reach down into the deepest part of me.

I like when the sun's rays caress my face.

It's then I know that I received my Father's grace.

I like the way the sand feels between my toes.

And the sound of the ocean when the waves roar.

I like the silence of my dark room.

Where there is no one to care for,

And nothing to prove.

I like the way my heart flutters when He draws near.

And how protected I feel in his warm embrace.

I like knowing that no matter where I may roam,

He's constantly with me wherever I go.

IMAGINATION

The whisper in the summer breeze.
The swaying of the trees' new leaves.
The howling of the ocean's tide.
All call to me by day and night.

The music as the raindrops fall.
The flowers dancing as moonlight calls.
And fairies singing round mushrooms tall.

A castle far upon a hill.
Horses grazing in nearby fields.
Shimmering lights from roaming streams.
These are many things I dream.

A mind is something not to waste.

Use it well, use it free.

It is a gift well meant to be.

To dream and wonder, to wander free.

To travel and see what no one has seen.

The mind can think of many things.

An imagination will set it free!

AWAKE OH DREAMER

You who are the dreamer of dreams
who in your state of sleep create many things.

In your thoughts to transcend form.
Limitless and powerful
with no boundaries and no walls.
In this state you have a taste
of life in all its fullness.

But only a taste is not enough,
when there is oh so much more.

Awake oh sleeper, oh dreamer of dreams
and bring with you those unlimited things.
From that world to this one,

that we may become one.

Awake oh sleeper, oh dreamer of dreams
and begin to reveal all you have seen.
For its source is not self,
nor is it a dream.
it's a vision from the future
of all you can be.

To exist in love,
to dwell in grace,
to even become that unlimited place.
Nothing is impossible, or too far out of reach.
If you'd only awaken from your state of sleep!

About the Author

Victoria (Tori) Martinez is a Latina poet, artist, and social changemaker rooted in the landscapes of the rural United States.

A proud first-generation college graduate, she writes from a deep well of lived experience and finds healing through creative expression.

Her work centers on belonging and the power of community, offering a voice to those who have often been left out of the conversation.

When she's not writing or painting, she's building bridges through storytelling, mentoring young leaders, and working to create spaces where all people feel seen and valued.

Out of the Ashes is her love letter to the universe.

Past publications include:

A Call to Awaken: A Collection of Poems, Vida Mestiza, 2025

The Geology, Ecology and Human History of the San Luis Valley, University Press of Colorado, 2020

Increasing Equity Through Place-based Education, Community Works Magazine, 2020

Students as Citizen Researchers: Giving Voice to the Community, Community Works Magazine, 2019

Three Dimensions of Placed-based Learning at Hispanic Serving Institutions, Excelencia in Education, 2016

"Two People". The Circle Book: A Conejos County Anthology, Alacrity House Publishing, 2013.

Visit the author's website for more information about her artwork, poetry, or to contact the author for public speaking requests at **vidamestiza.net**

www.ingramcontent.com/pod-product-compliance
Lightning Source LLC
LaVergne TN
LVHW090533110826
845146LV00003B/1081